Praise for Judy Hogan

This River

"*This River* holds our hands up to the magic in the dark moon with figurative language that pulls shards of tenderness from a world that is bloody with sting of sunlit longing and a psychic quest for redemption. These poems resurrect an ancient enchanted necklace worn by a *herstorical* aching that Judy Hogan bears into utterance. This collection is a meditation on time, memory, and the fleeting nature of life. Decoding the threads of aching and the heart of the language of two separate rivers is at the core of *This River*. These poems are a beautiful terrain forming the powerful backdrop for the magnificence of fragility.

Part primordial, part philosophical, powerful story inhabiting fluid boundaries between hearts, breaking the pedestrian parameters of space, time, and sensory experiences....*This River* is a lesson for weaving the baskets that are needed for carrying water to the Light."

~Jaki Shelton Green, author *Feeding the Light*

previous work

"...through her immersion in ancient Greek writing, Judy Hogan has gained the ability to connect many of the goddesses and female legendary/literary figures to the process of her life... she has written what may be a collection unprecedented in the renaissance of women's poetry in America."

~Virginia Scott, *Motheroot Journal (1977)*

"She doesn't indulge in a single excessive word, and the discipline of mastering Greek and Latin has helped hone her writing to a sharp edge."

~Charles Horton, *The Chapel Hill Newspaper*

About the Poet

Judy Hogan is a poet, former student of Greek philosophy at UC Berkeley (back "in the day"), founding editor of *Carolina Wren Press* and environmental activist. *This River* is Judy Hogan's sixth book of poetry, an epic love story written as the result of her work in writer exchange circles between Durham, North Carolina and Kostroma, Russia. "Holding true to her early doctrine of women speaking our truths, Judy's travels to and love of a Russian writer in this ancient village are revealed in *This River* with deep, inspired vulnerability". --*ed. note*

Judy Hogan

More Work by the Author

Poetry

Cassandra Speaking, 1977
Sun-Blazoned, 1983
Susannah, Teach Me to Love/Grace, Sing to Me, 1985
Light Food, 1989
Bobrinaya Dusha, 2007 Russian version *Beaver Soul*
Beaver Soul, 2013

Novels

Killer Frost, 2012
Farm Fresh and Fatal, 2013

Non-Fiction

Watering the Roots in a Democracy: A Manual on How to Combine Literature and Writing in the Public Library, 1989

The PMZ Poor Woman's Cookbook: Vegetarian Recipes for Survival and Health in the Menopausal and Post-Menopausal Years, 2000.

This River

This River

an epic love poem
by
Judy Hogan

Judy Hogan

Copyright © Judy Hogan 2014
ISBN-13: 978-0692320303
ISBN-10: 069232030X
Library of Congress Control Number: 2014956947

Published by *Wild Embers Press, Watersongs/Ariadne Books*, Ashland, Oregon and Taos, New Mexico. All rights reserved. Writer retains all rights to work. Use of any portion of this book should be requested through publisher. However, small quotes/excerpts are fine, with proper credit to writer. Artwork rights revert to artist.

Printed in the USA.
Wild Embers is a member of the New Mexico Book Association.
For special orders/education/artist discounts contact:

Wild Embers Press

www.wildembers.com
wildemberseditor@gmail.com

Cover/book design: antoinette nora claypoole.
Text typeface is Book Antiqua. Headings/titles are Goudy Old Style.

Interior drawing/graphic:
"Heart Leaves"
by Mikhail Fedorovich Bazankov (Михаил Фёдорович Базанков)

Book cover artwork:
"A Study" of the Volga River, Kostroma, Russia
by Sergei Rumyantsev (Сергей Румянцев)

This River

Contents

Preface	6
One	13
Two	16
Three	20
Four	24
Five	26
Six	29
Seven	33
Eight	36
Nine	40
Ten	45
Eleven	48
Twelve	51
Thirteen	54
Fourteen	57
Fifteen	60
Sixteen	63
Seventeen	66
Eighteen	68
Nineteen	74
Twenty	77
Twenty One	80
Twenty Two	82
Twenty Three	85
Twenty Four	87
Twenty Five	89
Twenty Six	91
Twenty Seven	95
Twenty Eight	99
Twenty Nine	102
Thirty	106

Judy Hogan

Preface

A few years ago in a poetry workshop the poet-teacher told us to write about our taboos. I already did that. I couldn't help myself. I had to write about what I felt, saw, thought. The hard part for me has been in publishing the writings that felt taboo, but gradually I've been doing it. *This River* is definitely such a book. The story in this epic poem happened more than twenty years ago when the United States and Russia had let go of the Cold War and encouraged their citizens to meet.

I had been working against the threat of a nuclear war in the 1980s. In 1989 the Sister Cities of Durham, North Carolina, began its official sister relationship with Kostroma, Russia, which had been closed to Americans during the Cold War. I joined Sister Cities and met Kostroma's Mayor Boris Korobov on his official visit to Durham to sign the agreement. He was approaching the Durham County library, as was I, who was teaching a class there that night. Apparently because I wasn't part of the group working with him, when I said, "Welcome, Russians," he came over to meet me because he wanted to meet someone who was not officially welcoming him.

We chatted for five minutes through his interpreter. I gave him a book I had published that

month (I was then the editor of Carolina Wren Press), and he gave me his card, saying, "Look me up when you come to Kostroma." At that time I couldn't imagine that I would ever go to Russia. It was, however, a mind-opening experience for me. I had grown up during the Cold War. My images of Russians were of cold, ruthless people. I told my students that night, and everyone I met, "The Russians are *friendly!*"

The following March I received a letter in Russian from the President of the Kostroma Writers Organization inviting me, and only me, to work with him on exchange visits of writers. Mayor Korobov had given Mikhail the book, *Watering the Roots in a Democracy: A Manual on How to Combine Literature and Writing in the Public Library*, as well as a letter I had written to the mayor saying I believed that international friendships helped prevent war.

I had planned a trip to Europe that summer of 1990 and would visit friends in Finland. I looked at a map. Kostroma was 250 miles northeast of Moscow and not that far from Finland. I wrote to Mikhail that I would like to visit and would bring my twenty-one-year old son with me. I received an official invitation. Our letters took one to two months to cross the ocean. We had no email then. He spoke no English, and I, no Russian.

Judy Hogan

A ten-member official delegation from Durham was also traveling to Kostroma at the same time. The chief organizer of that delegation was not happy that I, too, had an official invitation. I had to beg him to help me when he made calls to Kostroma. I had no trouble getting my visa and making travel arrangements by train from Helsinki to Moscow. I sent Mikhail my whole itinerary in Europe in the period before we would reach Moscow, where he was to meet us.

Then I got a telegram from Mikhail two days before I left the country, six words in Russian. I could find no one to translate it for me. With a dictionary and deciphering the Russian alphabet, I figured out the word *wagon*, but I didn't understand that in Russian that means *train car*. I wrote to him again, but that letter didn't arrive until after I had left Kostroma.

When Tim and I were in Finland I received a call from Mikhail's interpreter. They wanted to know the number of the train car. They did, that August day, find our car, and took us in a van back to Kostroma. One of the first things Mikhail told me was that I had a kind aura. All our verbal communication was through our interpreter, and she also became a friend. We were with them five days and were taken to see cathedrals, peasant homes, to meet the other Kostroma writers, and to the studio of a nationally known painter. Mikhail often talked about the Volga, the huge river which flows

This River

through the ancient city of Kostroma. He said that people once believed that if you put your hand in the Volga, you would be healed. We stayed in the Volga Hotel and could see the river from our window as well as a cathedral that was next door.

We met with Mayor Korobov in his office and heard from him that getting his citizens enough to eat was a problem. Tim suggested melting down the gold in the cathedrals. Neither Mikhail or the Mayor frowned or laughed. It was gently explained to Tim that they couldn't do that. The cathedrals were important, too. We also met Mikhail's wife and son, who was a little younger than Tim. We learned how close to nature Russians felt, how attached they still were to their villages, and how they had never stopped valuing the human soul, even under Communism.

I felt valued as a person and a writer. I was asked if I believed in God. I said yes, though I was not a church-goer. Through the years we worked together on exchanges and publishing projects, Mikhail often repeated the phrase "God is helping us." By *God*, he told me, he meant *Universal Mind*. Tim and I received extravagant gifts. If there were only two eggs, Tim and I should have them. They couldn't buy candy, but we were given candy and many other gifts.

When I left Kostroma, Mikhail and I had the mayor's blessing to start exchange visits between our writers, and I wanted to do everything I could to help my new friends who were having hard economic times. I had also fallen in love with this man who opened Russian culture to me and seemed my equal and my soul-mate in all the ways that mattered. I could tell that he loved me, too, but would never leave his wife and his sons. As we waited for our train back to Moscow, Mikhail said, "One day, Judy, we will each have a wing and we'll fly somewhere together."

    The love we felt and expressed covertly in letters was never consummated, but it became the fire that fueled our work together. We trusted each other. We argued and we adapted to each other's cultures as necessary. Our love spread out to so many people in the Kostroma Region and in the Triangle area of central North Carolina. Yet, even as I write this, it feels as risky to put it out there now as it felt in those early years. Perhaps it was the largest passion of my life, after my desire to write. It is the time, however to share this whole story. May it illumine other souls as it did ours.

Judy Hogan
Moncure, NC.
August 17, 2014

This River

For Mikhail

Judy Hogan

He:
Let it be better for both of us
that we got to know each other.

She:
You kept talking about this river...

This River

One

Every leaf of every resurrection fern is alive
and well-watered on the rocks along the
banks of the Haw. This river carries its
burden of mud and sloshes it over the
rocks; it cakes and cracks along the shore.
Today, as I watch the Haw rush recent
rains toward that ocean which you say
is the only barrier between us, I know
you are also saying there is no barrier.
Down here among the roots in my soul,
it is easy to agree. We are working
together beside our two rivers which,
though six thousand miles apart,
rush toward the same ocean. You
could swim across the Volga, and
I would be there. Yet I am here,
watching this river cover and water
her banks. They flourish; I flourish,
too. This new mud is fertile. At first
the leaves along the shore are painted
brown. Then sun dries them. Mud
peels off. New rains return their shine
to the bright leaves of summer, green

Judy Hogan

and gold, reluctant to fall. We have
August in October. Even the season
tries to stay where we were then.
Your absence is easier because the
leaves still shine. Sun celebrates
midday as if no chill had entered our
houses during the night; as if we had
not baked ourselves in the woodstove
toasted air.
              I have no names for this
place where I live now. Did you change
my heart into your beloved river, and
that's why, when I look at this mud brown
Haw, so intensely full of itself, I feel
your presence? You walk uphill from
that shore. Even your eyes are smiling.
You live with me on this hill, with its
trees and its blowing leaves. Some of
them are orange now. They flutter like
caught birds, eluding the wind. Fronds
of the cedar, the pecan's lower branches,
and the smooth, shining magnolia leaves
reach me the way your words do, stirring
the air between us with a barely moving,
gentle passion that turns suddenly bold

This River

and gusty. You are here where I am,
as near me as the sun and the wind, as
eager to move this air around me as you
were then to take the stairs two at a time
to show me you would keep pace, not
be left behind. Where I went, you
would follow. Because your heart had
been stirred, your feet would go quickly.

      We have need of the little stray winds,
which we harness to help us. But the
river's current is already ours. It runs
through our souls as one, my Haw and
your Volga. Both muddy, both healing;
both intent on their way to the sea;
running with a newfound power that
transforms every circumstance here
or there. We are hinged together by
ocean. That's why we are whole;
passionately healed, and well.

Judy Hogan

Two

I come to the river to feel the steady
running of the current that is in us
and between us, that is us when we
must be an ocean apart. Gold maples
shelter me, filter the sun as it rises
to its midpoint, haunts me where
I've settled to allow my love for you,
which lives in the depths of my days,
to float to the surface, greet the splashes
of orange and gold that lean over the bank,
solemnly reflected in the muddy water
even though it moves so fast today that
the colors blur and run. The sound
of the geese at some miles distant blurs,
too, yet drifts my way on the air that
is lazy and contented, not like the river,
which is urgent today just as it was urgent
when I was with you by the Volga. But,
no, here comes a wind to lift a few more
leaves which the rain left hanging, to shine
another day with holy light, like the candles
in a Russian cathedral, each one bright,
each one limited by time and its own
occasion, all of them together making the
miracle that is always and eternally gold.

This River

Trees hung with their flames help me
worship at this altar you taught me
was sacred. The brown water goes its
way prosaically, constantly. It's the gold
in the leaves which teaches me what such
a steady current is, in any life, no matter
what circumstances it runs past or what
faint trace of color it reaches upward
to hold in its hands and remember.
In the beginning your life doesn't show
many signs of transformation. True,
you are distracted by the internal fusion
going on, which is why you don't notice
what is happening along the shore.
Then you realize: nothing is the same.
Not only would you pick up everything
and go to him, but the enthusiasm in you
kindles in quite a new way. You heard
a man divide people into the sane and
the insane. "The sane," he said, "have
not faced death." I see my death in
these leaves I've gathered, the reds that
spread along their veins, the tips that
turn yellow and then, all too soon,
brown, which makes them part of the
ground again, part of the next season,
which begins as soon as this one ends.

Judy Hogan

You are constant. That's why, for the
first time in my life, I can be constant,
too. I don't need to hear the geese,
or see the long-legged herons flap
slowly, rhythmically by. All these leaves
could fall–they do fall even as I stare
at them–and a chill wind come to
rattle their dry forms. The river can
be harried with mud or peacefully
blue. The turtles I've often pinned
my hopes on could all dive below
the place where air breathes its life
into water. I need no symbols because
I've been given the source of symbols.
Your love holds me securely in my
place, in my world, which is coming
slowly apart as I watch, in order to join
itself with yours. Where you are the cold
has already made your fingers ache.
But I can wrap my red scarf around my
head and sit an hour among the golden
leaves as they transform themselves to
earth's cover and earth's food. I can
trace the current of my love to its source,

This River

and fear nothing. For you chose me,
earth accepted me, and the created
world sings over and over its hymn
to such a hectic current, muddy and joyful.

Judy Hogan

Three

What is it I want to tell you? I scarcely know.
I've come to sit on the little dock. Flooding
has anchored it in mud. The river drifts
past me. The water flowing over the dam
is barely audible. Only the water moves,
not fast enough to disturb the reflections.
The empty-armed trees root themselves
upside-down in the shallows near the
shore of the island. Mid-river the fringe
of their tops makes a lacy border. The cloud
cover descends below the surface as if
it plunged straight down, impatient with its
usual role of resting lightly. A narrow
channel of blue widens like a jet trail,
creates a highway above me, leading
beyond that line of trees.
                           Here below,
near where I sit, it stretches between these
mud flats and the dark shadow of the trees
which hug the other bank, anchored with
stones. The trees are bare now, yet dense
and dark; in close ranks; a boundary I can't
see through. I know nothing of what is
to be found on the other side. The island

This River

opposite is easier to think about, its rushes
at one end; its willows leaning their red
limbs my way; looking like giant water
striders about to skate off. When the river
floods, the island is covered with brown
water, and the wintering geese leave their
nests and the tender shoots of the rushes
they love to eat.

                    Four months since I met you.
August 2. About our time together you wrote:
"Our presentiments appeared to be accurate."
I had written: "At the fork of the road
higher up, I shall also know how to choose."
This fork has arrived for me now. I know
what I'll do.

                    As for you, you will visit
me soon. I know this in the way that
a log being pulled slowly by the current
knows that it will be swept over the dam
it can't hear yet. It has only its knowledge
of the motion which it is powerless
to change, sweeping it on toward its
destination. All the things we choose
are part of what is chosen for us.

Judy Hogan

       Two herons have landed. They
listen for fish as I sit here, also a statue,
listening for the beat of the poem, which
begins to rise from the slow coursing
of my blood. It leaps like a fish half
out of the water, with drops flying from
its tail, its silver side catching the light,
striking your eye so quickly that you
aren't sure what you saw. I've built
my life on such leaps–such sideways
flips in the air, such yearnings that pull
me into the swollen force of the current
that's impelled toward the sea.
       Out there
where there is only motion, it is easy
to believe your soul. Only one direction
is possible, whatever reflections come
and go. But the trail of blue through
the Southern sky I will take as my omen,
the sign I had needed to know, yes, I'm
at the fork higher up. I know where
I'm going and what I will do.
       We are
large-winged like the herons. We will play
in the air, leaning on capable wings.

This River

Then we will rest in the empty tree tops,
adding our big-bodied shapes to the fringe
of the trees at the center. The very fish that
we were will also be fish that we catch.
Every log shall be our resting place, and
every tree shall be our home. When the sun
returns to the sky, it will dance at the edge,
across water so black we fear to cross,
its glimmer beckoning, its radiance
connected to a pulse that resides in our
bodies, but also in our souls–a pulse that
stirs us both at the same moment, and
has made us, ineluctably, one.

Judy Hogan

Four

This river is fertile, but you would not know.
The fish have hidden themselves in the cool
mud. As if to show me I'm right, the sun
reveals himself and moves toward me on his
light-strewn path, across water, across land.
The water changes her brown, homespun cloak
for gold. She moves and swirls differently,
every gleaming fold of her gown outlined in light.
I am alone here. The beavers who have
reclaimed this river and the trees along
the bank are sleeping. The dog waits quietly
near the path for me to stand up and turn
toward home. She never settles as I do,
on some rock, until my body puts down
roots and the lapping water quiets my
soul. Will it be well with us? There is
so much space between. I pray to
the trees when I come here, my cheek
to their different barks, some rough,
some smooth. I pray, how I love you.
Do the trees near you hear my prayer
and whisper loving words when you
have put your cheek to their bark?

This River

Always and always I move among
difficulties, but my feet find their way.
Part of me is so certain that it doesn't
matter which way the wind ruffles the
water or how long the fish hide or when
the beavers wake and return to their labors.
Part of me is lulled right along with the
fish and sleeps in a beaver lodge, dreaming
of the gold light that crosses all the waters
of the world, all day, every day, day after
day. Now our days lengthen. We move
into the cold with spring already promised
us by the wind's warm breath. Light
begins its long, patient yearning toward
summer. The labors of winter will yield
us new colors in spring, and all the active,
practical green of summer. These twigs
already experiment this warm December
day with buds. All they want is sun.

Judy Hogan

Five

No light today, but life. The geese squawking
near the island, the snow goose among them.
The river reminds me: my life still holds time,
choices. The water stretches. The current is
belied by the wind, which blows my way.
The old is swept ashore, the debris from
living moments. All that remains are the
plastic drink bottles, the frame of a child's
sunglasses; sticks and logs the water has
smoothed and softened.
                          It is out of the sky
that the change will come. Some large bird
with huge wings slowly flapping will
suddenly announce the new. It's the first
time then for you to have your soul, your
very essence, loved and known; recognized.
It takes a like soul to do it. The snow goose
is happy near her favorite island. What else
has she journeyed for but to land here again,
for here there is the memory of what it means
to mate. It can't be wrong that I have tried
so many times, so many different ways.

This River

The river of love has poured and poured
from my heart, but it only pours the more
now when it hears the answer.
                          The river is so
quiet, it understates this truth. In me, too,
the river assumes more than it knows. I
learn my passion by the signs of its long-
lastingness. Such is the slender thread
to cross as our thread crosses. Yet the river
moves between us, carrying messages down
to the sea and across, and down another
river. What is ocean but the river that holds
the world in place and reminds it of eternity?
I didn't understand eternity till now. How
some moments last, their purity unquestioned
by the heart. I've had hints but never the man
saying with his whole heart (did he really say
this?) that he had searched all his life for
a woman, and I knew he meant like me.
This ties me to him as I've never let myself be tied.
Body and soul admitted instantly what took
my mind more time, more studying of stones
and rivers, the look of the sea and the sky
off Gower. Even now I keep that door shut
most of the time.

Judy Hogan

But the river with its grey
slates moving and the goose that makes
herself at home near the thick-growing reeds
and cattails with their tender shoots, speaks
loud enough when I sit quietly here on
the wet brown leaves and listen.

This River

Six

Memories are like fish: they rarely break
the surface. The trick is remembering
they're there, more active where there's no air,
where they least appear to move. The beavers,
too, do more than shows. I watch for signs
of their nocturnal labors, hold the bites
of wood and bark in my hands, distinguish
the pale orange of fresh wood from the grey
look that follows rain; think I see their
prints. Definitely deer have passed this
way, and raccoon. The beaver eludes me
like the fish do–so much so that, when
I did once see her swimming near shore,
it took me days to believe my eyes.
          Love is like this. Lulled among
our memories, it rarely shows itself,
and then we don't believe what we've seen.
Belief. In the absence of those chance flips
in the air. Belief. In the secret life of
the beaver to which she devotes her whole
intelligence in order to preserve her life,

Judy Hogan

her livelihood, and the lodge where her
children grow fat and strong; the lodge she
has hidden so well that I am baffled: I
can't read the signs, tell whether the old
lodges are newly inhabited; I think not.
Probably she has a new nest; has outwitted
me; has not only safety on her mind, but
longevity. She has learned from the river
winds how to fool the eye, how to blind the
heart that isn't pure and able to believe
what it has seen. The truth is always there:
it's in the way the current follows the
river bed, however dammed and held back
that flowing is. And the beaver's life leaves
proofs a trusting heart has no trouble taking
for evidence: a few fresh chips of wood,
and she knows the whole story. She can build
a world on one sentence she almost didn't
hear, which it took her months to believe.
The life of the river birds is known to her.
When they flap off, she knows by their not
having warned the other inhabitants, that
she is recognized, and that, after she has
settled on her chosen stone and begun
to trace the current of the poem across

This River

the page, that they will swing back in
to their favorite fishing shallows soundlessly,
keeping her form in mind, but not thinking
of her; their keen eyes more on the motion
of the water which implies fish are moving
their way.
                      She always has wanted proofs:
she has been so demanding, she frightened
those who loved her away. She would force
their secrets from them to have what she needed:
their pledge. Now she understands that she
must not drag the river for proofs; that every
day the river is new for her. Her memories are
not by any means inert, but feed and grow large,
Sometimes, when she least expects it, they leap
for pure joy into an air so foreign to them, so
risky, but ultimately attractive in its quiescence,
because it asks nothing, is simply there,
responsive to the wind's tricks and the sun's
showing off, not fooled by either. Her
intelligence is mobile and ingenious and,
like the air, it buoys up the creature or man
who breathes it deeply even into his very soul.
It holds the river smells—mud and old sticks,
dead fish and new eggs, the gradual salting
by those particles worn off rocks and swept

Judy Hogan

from earth. Water, mud, and air: they are our
universe. Without them we can't live, much
less invent our lives. For Life learns to hide
herself, not just for safety, but for the pleasure
of those leaps into the welcoming embrace of
air, so soft today, and comforting; as knowing
as old trees that it is wise to surrender
willingly to the teeth of the beaver, to allow
oneself to be as erotically alive as are
the fish, snug in their muddy beds.

This River

Seven

This river gives our life tone, force, beauty,
but we must not let it rule us. We do not
control the current nor the rains which intensify
its pace. Yet we must live with it or die.
I am awed by its relentless running, its mud
color that makes it look as if the last beech
leaves still clinging had dyed it their color.
The sky is blue today, but the urgent river
has no time for such foolishness. It has mud
to carry and leave thick and fertile over the
roots of trees and the crimson-eyed rose mallow
that is visible now only as bunches of upright,
dry sticks at the water's edge, with a few brittle
seedpods hanging on after the seeds have been
swept away.   I wanted this: the harmony, the
simultaneous recognition: you are who I thought
you were! It was and is a feast I had waited
a lifetime even to taste. I had forgotten my
normal needs would recur; my body notice when
a new man noticed me. He's here. For you I
hug the trees, but he has arms, which could
hug me back. I know you are more worthy.

Judy Hogan

But choosing you is like choosing eternity, and
I am still young.
           Penelope also had to do this.
The suitors, if rambunctious, were present.
She didn't want them. But there they were
wanting her. What could she do when her
own body yearned and took initiative against
her will, signaled to them that she might yield?
I might yield, too. He is gentle if distraught,
tender underneath his hostile practices. He
wants his chance. Then I remember: you also
must act. Even though I have chosen you,
I am still alone.
           We have work to do. We
can't give each other what we don't create
for ourselves. I promise to keep on choosing
the best. When I am here near the river,
the current whispers, "He won't let you down.
He waited a lifetime to find you. He is true.
He will find his way through as you will."
That's what the river teaches. The water
never stays in its bed, and yet it is true to its
current. Your heart knows the way. Follow
the green in the woods. Your life is in that
green. Brown dominates but green wins.

This River

The sun can change even this brown river
to a blue sea shimmering, its every slightest
motion christened by gold. Take brown, take
mud, take the restless, urgent water as part
of the deepest running in your soul you have
ever known, as the Snow Maiden's bubbling
blue heart, which you drank from because
you had already agreed to let him love you.
He'll do the rest, while you watch last year's
mallow bushes wave ever so slightly,
acknowledging the wind that hurried the
current but not ready to bloom yet. That
will take next season's sun and rain, the green
of the risen sap announcing: "I'm here now.
All's well."

Judy Hogan

Eight

Rivers deal in mud. We deal in love.
At our best our passion nourishes
and vivifies the good we are, the gifts
we give to help us speak of our
connectedness, how it is the same cloth,
rippling and then smooth, that we are
cut from, nay, the same mud. The Creator
also saw how the river loved her banks
with mud, took and gave constantly,
fertilizing with a prodigality wherever
she went, wherever she moved, intent
on life even in her reckless rush in
early spring when winter rains and
melting ice impel her she knows not
where, and creatures die because she
could not stop her rage once it began.
Driftwood rests in tree branches weeks
later. Dead leaves were caught out
of the roiling water at a height where
squirrels had intended nests and now
know better. But resurrection ferns
have sprung to life out of sheer rock.

This River

Decaying driftwood anchors vines
which will stretch up to tree limb
height next summer. We learn
to respect this river and her mud:
to work with her moods and changes,
not against her.
                    This river has two
incarnations. She is the Volga at night
not letting me sleep; making me listen
to the urgent message her moonlit water
carried me as I stood, half awake, my
heart's door swung open, fifty years of
sorrow held back, tears dry, because she
had had untold centuries of grief and
reminded me that I was young and loved;
that as long as rivers still move their mud
from place to place, we also can give
and receive love. Her other life is here.
She is the Haw, in sun. Her current has
dropped, her waters have quieted.
The dam holds her in such a trance
that she mirrors every tree and rock.
Every bird call can be heard for miles.
No killdeer sounds alarm without her
silence magnifying and sending forth
his cry liked daffodil trumpets proclaim

Judy Hogan

that yellow has arrived now to counter
grey. By holding still, she creates the
occasion, for love begins in knowledge
we at first want to ward off. Was it
my fear of all the difficulties or of
being so valued, so without parallel in
the experience of another? His whole
life he had looked for me? It took me
months to hear what my heart knew
the night the Volga woke me up. Every
tree has become my lover, and this
mud speaks loudly. I'm so far past
the whys I can't remember what
they were. It's only Life now, and
God–as I know It–and mud. The
message is everywhere: night there,
day here. Whatever the season or
the river's mood. She flows in my
heart now, another incarnation. My
stream runs faithfully, my current
loves you. I am too full of feeling to
stay in my banks, but every rock
will know my caresses, and the dead

This River

trees I carry from here will help new
vines and ferns feed there. I am brown
and solemn, with a green cast when
the day is still. Blue begins upriver,
pale but full of self-knowledge,
moving this way. Serenity is possible
because of mud.

Judy Hogan

Nine

In a bottle I found washed in by the river
I have put four yellow narcissus. They are
my sun today on a winter afternoon. Below
this vase on the window ledge are the birch
shoes you gave me. Beside them is the
open book with its blank pages, which
Victor gave me. Its stone is from Siberia.
On the other side of the shoes is a small
gift from Galina, a painting of *Berendevka,*
the film set for "The Snow Maiden,"
which you took us to visit. There was no
snow then. We sat in the shelter of a
house that had no inside. We made
the inside live with our conversation.
You and my son talked about fathers
and sons, while I listened and Natasha
translated. I learned that day how you
have mastered self-restraint when
people infuriate you. My son talked freely;
how he wanted to punch the man who
had been rude to your son the night
before. You admitted he had made you
angry, too, but you remembered he was
an old man. I knew then that you had
often had to master your passions, also

This River

that you had never killed them off. You
knew how he felt. Whatever winter
there is there, bleak, with grey skies,
bitter cold, ice, the land held white
in its iron grip, I know there is also
a room in your life where you keep
yellow narcissus, their trumpets as
lasting as white Siberian stone.
Ice stiffens them sometimes, and
they fall. If it snows, you must bring
them indoors. But year after year
they thrust their way through the grass
at the foot of the hill, large clumps
of them. As early as January, they
announce the return of the spring.
    I think of Achilles, wandering in
the meadow where the good dead wait.
Achilles among the daffodils, wishing
he were a servant in his father's house.
He didn't want to lord it over all the
dead. Daffodils are my lifeline. They
endure the sleet and ice, the death we
all must give.
        At the bottom of the hill
there was a house once. Buttercups
brightened its yard. Now they brighten
my winter walks down the hill to the

Judy Hogan

river. My heart is suddenly light.
The sun lies scattered like leaves dazzling
a surface the wind rakes, then turns
to gold, while the pure blue of the sky
holds its exuberance in check. Where
has that leaden sky gone, all those
days of impenetrable muddy water? Why
now is there as much blue rising out of
the river's depth as I could ask for,
as much gold conversion singing the song
the daffodils sing, only louder, as if fluid
gold swept sparkling toward me were
the last piece of evidence I needed to
know that you love me, and not fleetingly,
which would be understandable, given
our circumstances? No, it's as though
there were yellow narcissus blooming
right out of the pages of your letters.
I could put them beside the little shoes
of birch. They would be happy there
with the polished Siberian stone and
the old bottle I put flowers in. You
have found a way to pass right through
the language barrier, with my translator
being no wiser, and get me your
messages, like yellow narcissus

This River

first poking up their green thumbs
through dead leaves and matted grass
roots. Then a bud forms at the stalk's
end. As it lengthens, the yellow
trumpet opens: "Here I am again, a sun
you didn't expect to find that has
waited underground for these six months.
And now I must declare my love."
        This must be why, at odd moments,
a sudden happiness lifts itself up in my
soul like the daffodils lift their bonnets
from the plainest possible soil. I don't
understand where it comes from. I've
never had underground vibrancy before.
Once I would have shouted it to anyone
who would listen and then captured its
rhythm in a poem. In the end I'd be
left with nothing but poems. This time
the river sends me a different message.
Winter skies do not deter this blooming,
nor does the river hesitate to startle me

Judy Hogan

with gold, reminding me that my heart
harbors daffodils now, and the river
radiance is like a song which repeats
itself, without my starting to sing,
over and over, without sound.

This River

Ten

My cheeks are cold, but today the tree bark
is warm. Another metaphor I live inside.
When I hug these solemn trunks, I hug you.
On wet dark days their bark is cold, but
today, when winter sends one last chilling
blast, ruffles the river into waves that
slap the old dock hard and liven up the
geese on the island–they go swimming,
call loudly to one another, and delay
migration–I reassure myself that spring
won't go back now by hugging trees. Does
their sap keep them warm? My blood
warms as I think and walk. In the middle
of the road into the Boy Scout camp
I see the Cullowhee lily putting up her
leaves, the violets already purple under
their leaf curls. The cardinal is right;
the wind is wrong. The limbs outlined
against that grey canvas, winter, show
faintly the evidence: new leaves.

Judy Hogan

      I return to August, those five days
which set in motion a transformation I
live more easily than I believe. My
breasts are Russian now. They like to
think of you. The life force turns my blood
warm when I'm there near you or you walk
slowly up this rutted road beside me.
      I come back, warmed, to my woodstove,
put on a log from the sweetgum limb that fell.
The tree itself is too big for me to hug.
When I hug the small ones, I wonder if
they're strong enough to carry my messages
to Russia. Maybe burning a log of sweetgum
will propitiate the gods. My body cools as
the room warms.
      You will sit here. We will
speak Russian this time. I will hear you say,
"Da" again. The stove will be cold.
The ceiling fan will move summer's heavy
air. All the yellow narcissus will be dry
then, their stems curled like old paper.
I'll put orange trumpet flowers, daisies,
Queen Anne's lace, and honeysuckle

This River

in a vase on the woodstove. We will
hear the cardinal singing her dawn song
and the mourning doves lamenting the
August air before it is full light. We
have talked all night. Our coffee is cold,
our eyes warm.

    We walk together toward
bed, toward sleep. The cardinal has
forgotten his winter song, full with his
presentiments of spring.

Judy Hogan

Eleven

Summer begins in March with fully revived
resurrection ferns and the pale green runners
of honeysuckle vines spreading upwards
from the forest floor. Bluets and violets
open in the woods, crocuses in my front
garden. My heart is afraid of summer. It
knows before I do what I will suffer then.
My knowledge and my wisdom took me
to stand on the doorstep of your heart, and
when you welcomed me, I had no choice
but to enter. But then I stumbled and fell.
I was afraid of the house I had entered.
I am still afraid though I'm trying to learn
my lesson from the shrilling of the spring
frogs, the faint protest of the geese who
have moved upriver today. From the green
response of the vines, first covering the
brown floor, then climbing.   Life has gnawed
away all my limbs but this one. If you don't
love me, as I believe you do when the sun
floods the grey water and every motion
forward is bathed in light, as if every dip
it made brought light up from below,

This River

as if it weren't the solitary sun's work,
but a hidden pool of silver in the depths
which the waves found as they moved, but only
when they moved forward–there is no going
back; if you are not the reason my days gild
themselves from below consciousness as I
dip my pen in ecstatic vision after ecstatic
vision and write my way toward you, I know
I will fall again, and this time the wound
won't heal.
              I can accept paradox and a territory
so unknown that everything I have learned
from all my previous sufferings is like having
your whole life reduced to one handful of sand
and then seeing the world you must now
construct with that small number of grains
appear before you. But every grain I am
holding is one I individually discovered and
paid for; every grain is no one's but my own.
For each one I am willing to suffer again.
I know I can't have proofs ahead of time.
It's only a question of mustering courage.
        The geese swim up, curious. They must
see my dog at the water's edge, and me, too,

Judy Hogan

behind these trees, with my red scarf on
against the wind. Do geese swim this close
in order to answer the soul's questions?
They speak now that they are swimming
away. They stayed awhile first, staring and
not speaking, their bodies buoyant like a
fleet of small ships, the water moving them
more than they moved themselves. I have
my answer, though I understand neither their
silence nor their speech. If geese come
to answer my soul's questions, I am right
to fill my other hand with courage and
continue to walk forward, learning to
balance again on both feet.

This River

Twelve

How easily these trout lilies put their leaves out,
then slender stalks with blooms. For such a
brief time they hang their yellow bonnets. Then
yield this fragile beauty happily in a warm
spring wind. March finds them almost finished
with their yearly labor, uncomplaining that their
petals had so short a time to live, are withered
now, and soon to be released by this wind that
lifts dead leaves they hide among. They have
held their place for centuries among these old
grey rocks. The wind may ravage them and
even tug off their disguise for all they care: seed
awaits warm air and the scattering hand that
they know will come.

                        Here in Equinox Time,
I, too, admit to seed. My love lives in poems
now, its yellow petals curled back with simple,
confident, fleeting grace. I don't need stone
to prove to me this lasts: further, there are
smooth green pods to which the withered
petals shyly cling. But in the Universe's heart
I've come to know these flowers also live.
Their death is what is fleeting, their life is
more eternal than mere stone, for they sing
to us when we are worried. They remind us

Judy Hogan

we are beautiful and touch strings that
waited years for music to begin; they stir
awake the knowledge we have carried
unaware until we learned it for ourselves
because a flower we had not believed in
dared to put out petals as easily as these
trout lilies always do.   We human beings
may have lost our kings but not their ermine
and their gold. It flourishes here on this
forest floor and also in the souls of those
who love and let love live. There kings
and queens will reign; there all is stately;
doubts don't enter in; power is given
freely because safely held.
                              The river has
this wisdom in her running when Winter makes
his blustering retreat north and the geese begin
to practice leaving, too, their cries jubilant as,
with their long necks outstretched, they skim
the river's still rumpled grey silk quilt. The
turtle sticks his nose out: what is going on?

This River

He hangs floating, warmed by sun, while he
looks around, then dives away when he sees me
watching. The bluets laugh at him, and the
little green mosses wave their grasses with
the formal and dignified confidence of a
late arriving trumpeter just in time to announce
the king and queen. Here they are: before me
on this hillside with its crop of mottled stoles,
gold lily bonnets nodding. The traveler in me,
finding her way along a path she learns so
slowly and has cause to fear, takes in this
glorious court in session, these wise and
faithful flowers, happy to light up a forest
floor, if only for one week. More just and
more eternal than a six months' winter
with his stony doubts.

Judy Hogan

Thirteen

What is this mystery, this green that holds
us one when we are half a globe apart?
It rises like these leaves are rising:
ancient ritual of return. My love for you
also resurrects itself. The rain that poured
on roofs, washed dirt and gravel downhill,
swelled creeks, moves urgently downstream
today, floods all the ravines, and covers
the islands. It will leave mud behind for
summer flowers, autumn grapes, and the
shoots the geese come back for every year.
    I have six months to wait for you.
The leaves will be dying then. The river
will carry autumn rain, and when it quiets,
we will see the yellows on the farther
shore turn gold, then upside down. My life
is upside down now, too. I must believe in
love that has no sacred ground it calls its own;
no garden. I do not wish to claim another's
ground. Yet I wish for this, the best that I
have known. The little green leaves on
this forest floor reassure me. Every year
they let themselves exist again. They wear
their tender green with an insouciant air.

This River

Some wear flowers, too. Even a dogwood
once uprooted in high wind, still bears her
leaves, her pale green petals which will
whiten as the days pass. Were there no
cruelty, no separation, no loss, this green
would not so comfort me. Isn't it because
human life has tragedy written into its plot
that we cling to the lines we already know
by heart? They have worked for us before,
held back the losses we would do anything
to ward off. If only we could hold back
that curtain like Athena held back Dawn
for her reunited pair. Loss was all around
them; for us, too. Yet a firm hand leads
us toward our bed and keeps our vows
intact until the gods allow return. In me
something has waited all these years to do
what I do now; sustain belief with only
images to guide me: memories that work a
miracle when I'm not looking. My twisted
foot walks normally again, and I have hope
of finding blue when right now the river's
message is of brown, more brown. Belief
is hard though these leaves make it look
so easy. They are new, yet they take their
rightful place as though they'd never left it.

"Of course, we come again. What did you expect? He also comes because you keep on summoning belief. Human beings suffer, true, but also heal. You carry proofs. You passed through a narrow space, turned upside down, and lived again. You are resilient now. Your blood and spirit know a single dance. You let Truth rule, surrendering first your will. Content yourself with green unfurling. Allow your happiness its blind but knowing way where pain has made a path. Then yield to what, though new, is also right, and good."

This River

Fourteen

Yesterday the geese came calling. They were
swimming mid-river when my dog and I
walked up; I settled on this rock to watch them,
and they swam toward me, talking the while.
They stayed within a dozen feet of me, floating
one way, then turning, as a body, and paddling
upstream in order to continue their covert
looking me over. Is there some obvious
explanation? Someone feeds them, and they
decided I might, too? Or do they hear the
question in my soul and flock to answer?
Perhaps their souls yearn to hear my answers
to their questions?
                                        Two fishermen are
drifting along the bank on the other side,
and no geese. I'm trusted by these geese.
I belong to their private world, as they
have belonged these years to mine. Our
first hot day. Every tree has its first shade
of green, most with a yellow cast. The river
wavers with a little wind. The colors are
fainter over there, like an Impressionist
painting. Trunks look like poles; the greens

Judy Hogan

blur with the brown water. When the wind
picks up, the whole painting is gone. A big
fish jumps in the air near me. The fishermen
don't see it. The trees hang out their tassels.
Summer works on her painting before
spring has finished reveling in chlorophyll.
The geese know my secrets. The fishermen
have no way of suspecting the presence of
geese. I see deer and raccoon tracks
in the mud. In another five years maybe
they will drink while I'm present. Why
should twenty-five geese trust me? Why
do you? Most people do, and those who
are wary are wary of the way people turn
to me, confident they're safe. So much
trust can be unnerving to witness if you
don't understand how it's done. I don't
understand myself why you love me or
these geese do. I'm loved despite, or
because of, my errors. The fish are jumping
everywhere but where the fishermen are.
Why do they jump near me? Maybe, like
the geese, they've gotten to know me.
They read my heart. You read my heart
that first day. You said I had a kind aura.

This River

Is that what the fish read? In this river world there's a conspiracy against intruders, and I've been taken into the plot. The little spring beauties and the violets keep blooming. Is it because I pass them so often, marveling? Is it my love of the geese and the fish that brings them out to see me. Is that why the big river turtles rise to have a look before they dive away? I miss the geese this early April morning. There are events that occur only once and satisfy so quietly, so deeply that their pleasure lasts for a lifetime.

Judy Hogan

Fifteen

In me, too, green. Powerful, clear, insistent.
Never in my life has so much love possessed me,
stored so mysteriously in my roots–every
fine hair vibrating so that the arrival of your
letter is all it takes to transform me. The
vitality we call sap in trees, ichor in gods,
eros in people takes me. I am more changed
than this forest, which merely turns bright
green. Green is an understatement compared
to what happens to me.
                            Yet I understand that
I can't yield to you unless we both give
our souls permission. My body wants to
express this, but the fire leaping again into
view out of coals that had seemed dead is
the soul's blaze. Love never was so pure
in me. Passion, not lust. I can yield up my
need to touch you, but my mind persistently
tells me that this, too, will come. No, it
isn't the green so much as the river that
teaches me. Its mud-brown water contains
all my agony. I give up my pleasure easily
for your sake. It returns two-hundred fold.

This River

The raging spate where spring rains have
swollen creek and the skies have emptied
their buckets steadily for days–is nothing to
the force of my love when it moves me.
           In this place where I'm sitting, it doesn't
matter what you do or choose or what exactly
happens between us. You have let me know
that you think of me when a fine rain falls
and when the sun is bright and pouring down
sunshine. I will suffer. To be out of your
arms for one hour would be too long, but
I don't have any promise except in my
soul's deep and confident knowing that I
will ever be in them. What is suffering
but learning to change your life? Adjusting
to a higher, better way to live? It is so
simple and so easy. It's like water touching
the rock over and over to remind it:
"I'm here. I'm here." That's all I need.
The knowledge you're there, and here.
You're always here where I am, oh,

Judy Hogan

far one, oh, near one. I yield to nature's knowledge, her green wisdom, her floodtide of mud. Carry me where you need me, oh, Life. If love is like this, I'll go. I'll go.

This River

Sixteen

In four months you will sit on my favorite rock,
smell the river, see raccoon prints in the drying
river mud; stare at the sun caught in the shallows;
hear the dog lapping, let the tide of light the wind
blows shoreward enter your soul. The hearts-a-
busting bush will hang with pink pods and orange
seeds then. Now they are small, green, and fuzzy.
The leaves will be yellow and red as well as green.
We will watch them fall upside down and float
away on the slow river tide. If it has rained,
there will be green resurrection ferns; if not, we
will know that their dead look means survival,
not that they aren't alive.
                                 I understand everything
you say and what you don't say, too. I am ready like
the ferns, alive or dead, as needed, to survive or
to flourish. The caked mud, drying and cracking,
still damp, reminds me of all that the river carries
within it.
                This river has changed my life. It runs
in me whether I'm sitting beside it or not; whether
I come to breathe its clean river smell or not.
Mud, water, and life. They smell clean, though

Judy Hogan

they look dirty. So, too, the river in me. I know
now it's my soul. All my love runs there.
The current is steady and strong, a river in its
middle life with its vital tide. It teaches me
to love as my last child taught me to trust my
breasts to feed her. The river doesn't answer
my questions, but it continues its buoyant
motion, carrying my soul along with it. Finally
I comprehend: I am a river. I must do what
the river does, move on and on. I must love
my banks. Then all will be well in my depths
and also in my recurring tide of light. This river
won't fail us. She remembers what we forget.
She carries with her what we leave behind. She
lifts us up when we feel heavy. She reveals
her heart when we are frightened. Courage
is easy for her. She dissolves her fears like
the mud, and then her motion, her every
gesture, transforms them to light. What we
don't understand floats toward us,
astonishing the watchers, their feet braced
on the rock where sticks have drifted;
their skin caressed by the wind that hurries
the light toward them. Light carriers
like we are recognize the river's message

This River

when it arrives. Read the caked, drying
mud for signs; interpret the flowers of
the button bush leaning toward the mud
brown water, as thirsty. We are safe behind
a screen of cottonwoods, but what is safety
to a river? She wants to love her way home.

Judy Hogan

Seventeen

From here the only path leads up.
The heights beckon, light held in their
bright green containers, thin, translucent,
their edges sharp and perfectly formed;
their holes and spots don't matter.
They understand me and where I'm
headed. The brown river with its beads
of breath from fishes understands, too,
and the hummingbird which entered
my cove because the bright colors
in my shirt made him think he saw a
flower. Sweat pours down my back.
I walk well now, but my foot remembers
falling. Belief in this river in all her
phases; her pulse of life intact;
her bubbles rising; her mud moving;
light at an angle turning her white;
is all I have. I am a butterfly now,
queen of the spaces between the trees,
monarch of all that I own: my life,
my soul, my will, my choices. They all
depend on this river and her mud,
this river and the life she carries within

This River

her; this river and her light. First beads,
then motion. The bubbles float downstream;
the evening light moves in like a second
river, white and calm; my soul is in that
light, gentle and clear. The brown daytime
river has questions. She suffers. She
needs to know what to do. But the evening
river contains all the answers the soul
ever needs. The answers are wordless,
confident, a white sheet of water visible
offshore between dark trees.

Judy Hogan

Eighteen

"Growing in Spirit"

*He who hopes to grow in spirit
will have to free himself from obedience and respect.
He'll hold to some laws
but he'll mostly violate
both law and custom and go beyond
the established, inadequate norm.
Sensual pleasures will have much to teach him.
He won't be afraid of the destructive act:
half the house will have to come down.
This way he'll grow virtuously into wisdom.*

--C.P. Cavafy, translated by Edmund Keeley

My soul is all I have left to give you.
Everything else is perishable, and, anyway,
very little belongs to me. I do not own
my house or my garden. I have to my name:
an old car with a new engine, which
is not yet paid for; a couch, some beds,
a few chairs, some old tables; odds and
ends of dishes and pans, most of them

This River

historical. I have baked the children's
birthday cakes in the same pan for
nearly 30 years. Nor have I become
a household word in America. So I do
not even have that asset. Locally a few
thousand people have heard of me.
She stirs passion for good or ill; is loved
and admired by some, feared and hated
by others; it comes of learning to use power,
to take one's place in the world in a way
that matters.

But what I do have is my soul.
It's a Russian soul, or, at least the Russians
I have met seem to understand what I'm trying
to do and be in my soul better than most
people I know. As do you. That's why
and how you became necessary to me.
Everything else I can do without. It's your
soul's understanding of my soul that I must
have, and my understanding of yours which
I want to give you, as well as I can.

What a puzzle my soul is, even to me.
I have it only insomuch as I heed its commands.
This, too, is a gift. Only an old soul knows
when to make you listen. Most of the people
I know never hear what I hear; never see
the signs. The quiet brown river flowing

Judy Hogan

past does not reassure them as it does me
that the universe still says "yes" to the rock
where my soul has come out. The single red
leaf I pick up reminds me that you
will be here soon when all the leaves are
red and yellow. My fear is balanced with
joy now. I will cross over whatever the
circumstances are that arise, that I can't
foresee, just as I have for years now
found a way to cross over the runoff creek
in my woods. I'll step on a root that grows
out into the water. I'll pull a fallen log
over to make a bridge. I'll hold onto the
nearest tree branch. And if I get my boots
in the mud, I'll clean them off and dry them
out. It's my life. My soul. My gift of my
life to leave behind me. I see the landscape
of my life as a whole now. I don't know
the future in detail, but I feel its presence
in my soul. I have learned enough to risk
whatever I need to and do what I must do.
I have had the good luck you wished me:
I am building a human soul.
                              What, you
may ask, were the necessary conditions?
Can I describe them? Do I even know?
My soul was taken seriously by my parents,

This River

though, when I began to decide things for
myself, they were startled. They did not
recognize the fruit that had formed itself on
their tree. I have refused to do what made
me feel like I would die inside if I did it.
I was foolish sometimes. My soul forgave me.
It asked only for life, not for perfect behavior.
I have learned risk. I have given up happy
endings. I have stopped trying to coast.
Every day I wrestle with guilt. I have guilt.
Every day I work against the deadline I feel,
which is the end of my life, though my soul
tells me it's thirty years away. Thirty years is
not very long for what I still have left to do. I
feel terror a lot. I feel joy more. Passion runs
in my veins along with my blood--perhaps
there's more passion than blood by now.
Perhaps my blood is changing to the ichor
that belongs to the gods. It wakes me up.
It rushes me here and there. It makes me fight.
I do things on impulse if they're important.
I'm not deeply afraid of anything human any
more, though I still dread people's hate, and,
as I can, I evade their games that try to make
me what I'm not. I give of myself less foolishly
and I hoard my time, my resources, my money

Judy Hogan

for the sake of the big gift I'm giving. I think,
when I am besieged by the need of another,
"No, I won't hold your hand, but I'll write
a book for you that will help you more than
holding your hand will." I told one friend--
it felt cruel, but it was what I could actually do--
that I would help him live, but I wouldn't help
him die. It took him some months, but now he
writes to me nearly every day, and I answer.
I leave it to other people to tend to their
souls. Not many like this. I'm not that virtuous
or well-behaved. Sometimes I do deserve the
reproofs that feel humiliating to me. But I also
understand that people fear my power.
I suffer, and then set the suffering aside.
I feel self-pity fleetingly, if at all. There
is too much at stake. I am a grain of sand
staying intact when the world has more
and more devices, subtle and not so subtle,
for breaking the edges of the soul, crushing
to dust individual grains of sand. I refuse
that crushing. I will leave sharp edges in the
consciousness of others to help them refuse
that inglorious an end. I, too, will be crushed
in time. I've accepted that. Steamrollers
abound. But not by choice. Not willingly.

This River

And not before my edges have made an impression.
        Your love is all I ask, and my own soul's flowing response.
        Run, run, our souls, carry us seaward! Save our planet, our people, our life, our rivers and birds and trees, and all the little wild flowers that artlessly stand in their royal bonnets along the river's banks. For them to bloom once a year for a few days is enough. For me, to leave a few words that prick like the diamond edge of the sand, is enough. I do it for me and for you. Love helps me do it. Love is the trout lily of our souls, its bonnet gold, its beauty uncontested, its power eternal.

Judy Hogan

Nineteen

In me is certainty. In the river at an early
evening hour, the light whitening its muddy
depths, is certainty; in the beaver sleeping
under the bank where he has almost
gnawed the sweetgum tree enough to fell it
is certainty. In the hearts-a-busting bush
turning its seedpods pink and its seeds
orange in honor of your fall arrival is
certainty. In the cottonwood seedling
that has rooted itself in a cracked rock
is certainty. In the evening swallows
darting for insects as the day declines
and cools, there is certainty. In the massed
green of the trees on the other bank,
which stretch their reflections almost
the whole way across the river, there
is certainty. In the sky, pale, the clouds
breaking to let the last blue of the day
show itself, and the sun's light wink a
few times before it vanishes behind the
trees, there is certainty. In the big fish
startling the silence, with his tail flapping
as it hits the water, there is certainty.

This River

In you, too, I feel the same certainty
even without your words. I feel it
when I must wait months for a new
message. Then where does doubt begin?
It begins when I try to explain. "Then
don't explain. Allow miracles. Permit
delight. Take in mystery whenever and
for whatever reason it comes upon you.
Didn't the sweetgum stars tell you as much
last night? They were there all the time.
You have lived near their tree for five
years, but you never looked before. Pay
attention. That's easy enough, and you do
know how. You figured out where the
beaver was after months of puzzling.
You know the man wants to give you his
heart, and will. He's very determined
on that. Once no amount of evidence
would satisfy you. None of the others loved
you enough to give you his whole heart. He
has yours, right? So why do doubts buzz
and disturb this serenity you are inheriting.

Judy Hogan

Other people won't prevent it, damage it,
or understand it. They can't. He'll sit here
on this rock beside you. You'll show him the
hearts bursting open. He'll put his arms
around you and kiss you, because his heart
has opened as easily as their bright pink pods.
All the seeds are orange, and they all belong
to you. The herons will coast in, long bodies
gliding, to the shallows where fish rise to
the surface for evening flies, and you will
watch them spearing and swallowing fish.
Their aim never misses. They are certain, too.
The Universe breathes out its certainty.
Open your pores."

This River

Twenty

As soon as they can, things grow. Give
them a little mud, even caked and hard
on a rock, and they're off. Later their
leaves will be tattered, half-eaten,
exhausted, but they are filled with delight.
They have lived out the pattern they
carried in their light-sensitive cells.
They know no regret. Even loss is part
of the joy of having lived completely.
        A day comes in September when they
understand why. Sun warms but does
not burn the air; a breeze lifts their
leaves, and they look like flags flapping
in a steady wind. The fish come in
near shore to play in the warmed shallows.
A sandpiper, blown inland from the sea,
struts bouncily around a rock shelf
hunting the mussels whose living odor
scents the air as it stirs over the water.
Everything alive is graceful and at ease
today. Every why is understood. The
heart has all its questions answered.
After all, if joy is given, one takes joy,
just as mud was given–sloshed heavily

Judy Hogan

over the bare rock, where it stayed,
where it meant fertility, where it nourished
the seed that fell. Life moves forward,
stepping from one possibility to the next.
I have seen the stepping stones. That's all.
My soul has had the canniness to notice,
to plant itself in the proffered mud, and
to grow. This love lives. I have helped
it live.
           Once these trees, vines, grasses,
the hearts-a-busting bush, did not exist here.
The river gave them life just as it gave me
love. You can't make it happen. But when
Life opens all her treasures in September,
you open your arms and gather them all in.
You let your soul hear what She's saying.
You need luck. Luck will be given. You
need disguise. Your love will hang as safely
among its leaves as the cucumbers do. You
need time. Time will be given. You need
self-control. You will have it. Life blesses
you. Eternity moves in you like the river moves.
The current is always there, but sun and wind
distract the eye. You are conscious of it all

This River

now. Don't forget. Your memories are
deeper and steadier than the wavering water
marked silk tide that leaves its shapes
on the sand.

Judy Hogan

Twenty One

Do birds come when you need them?
For me they do. I can't always read
their messages, but I know they're
telling me, "Yes, yes, you're doing
the right thing." I don't know how
they hear me or why. The more often
it happens, the deeper the mystery.
There's a heron now in the trees
over my head. He announced
himself with a squawk and stayed.
Some small birds I don't know flew by
just before that, shouting something
urgent into the wind, and I know it
wasn't that they feared me, or they
wouldn't have come so close. Surrender
of will is the secret. Then the birds
come. What is already given to me
brings all the birds with their urgent
cries, their calm, deliberate presence.
My worries do not disturb a heron's
midday fishing.   We do not get to see
ahead of time Life's plan or what
our shape will be for others when it
has settled into a firm outline when

This River

we're gone. For us there is only
the movement forward as through
a forest where the path is overgrown
or never has been made. You go where
the spaces big enough for you let you
pass. When they won't let you by, you
turn another way. You are more surprised
when you do pass by than when they stop
your motion forward and you must revise
your plan. If you ask only for what you
need, it will be given. Astonishment
gives way to consciousness of grace.
If you want your soul and body to be
filled with light that flows over you
like a river moves up the rocks it
knows by heart, you must trust the gifts
of the spirit and not refuse them.
In the end your outline will be
visible at great distances because
of the light you learned how to contain.

Judy Hogan

Twenty Two

To write and to love: my life tasks for
the years left me. It sounds simple.
It means giving close attention, making
an extra effort every single day. Every
day I lose is gone. "Water over the bridge,"
my grandma said once to console me.
But it never returns, the water that
passes over. It is "our chance" passing,
too. We must choose carefully every
day, balance within ourselves and within
the day our needs, the needs of others,
our most urgent tasks, and what we will
let flow past us, never to return.
                              The river's
morning stillness promises more. But I
know the current is constant, whatever
the wind on the surface implies, making
it look like we can return to the places
and the times where we have already been.
There is truth in that backward flowing water.
In memory and in art we do return to what
matters, to what deeply impressed itself
on the inner retina, carved itself into the
walls where our soul makes itself at home.

This River

Time continues to stream forward. These
moments of contemplation are like frail
leaf boats dropped from trees that tilt
out over the water. They float upstream
briefly before the inexorable stream calls
them toward ocean.

A very old turtle
knows this better than anyone. She floats
to the surface to breathe, to take her
bearings, to spend a few hours in the sun,
drying and healing her shell. But most
of her hours are spent in the river's depths
fighting, using, outwitting the current
that marks and defines those depths.
There are no illusions there. The river's
passion is clear, which way it moves,
and what it intends to do.

Two things we
human creatures find hard: to know what
we feel and then to accept that knowledge.
Here is where the Universe intrudes: like
it or not, we feel what we feel. Our choice
is to know and to rejoice. For those who
navigate Life's stream, the room the Soul
dwells in is calm and beautiful. Days
are given in which there is nothing that
doesn't make sense. The water shimmers

Judy Hogan

with the yellows of early fall; the dark green
depths are turbulent with fish-felt rather
than seen. Everything is possible born
into time, alive and then lost, leaving
its traces, its record, its frail craft beached
at long last on a distant shore.

This River

Twenty Three

Does the holy always come into our life
in the heart of a conflict? I think so.
The heron, his feet in the cold water,
wading and calling throatily to the fish,
agrees with me. "You will suffer,"
he says. "The rain falls, doesn't it?
So will your tears. But joy enters inevitably
when you are this clear, this content with
what life pours out and into your arms.
       "Like those wild grapes you found.
Hundreds of them ripening on vines low
enough to reach by bending down the
little tree they clung to. Keep asking your
heart what to do. Then you'll know.
Every cove where the water runs shallow
and the fish swim in it has a heron stalking,
one foot at a time, determined on his dinner.
       "He comes for you. Take what is given
to a pure heart, a spirit cleansed by the tears
you have shed and will shed. There is no
end to the tears, but joy is in them. Like
light turning muddy water pale yellow or
as blue as the sky over your head, eternally

Judy Hogan

confident and serene, as you are, as you
will be. It is the gift the gods gave you:
your willingness to take in this love
and give him your beauty back. Let
nothing disturb that clear gift, that joy
which he'll see in your eyes every time
he looks at you. It will feed his spirit
as well as it feeds yours. This love is
given like the sun and the rain. Turn
your face to its blessed light, bathe
yourself in its *unwardoffable* * tears."

*unwardoffable is a poet created word from a Greek phrase used in battle depicting the idea that you can't "ward off" or keep away the enemy.

This River

Twenty Four

And what is love? This feeling I have for you
which defies my understanding and insists
that I yield to it, throwing me to the ground,
if necessary, to make its point?
                                                    It begins in
the heart and moves other places. For over
a year it has claimed all of me, though you
were six thousand miles away. Now in two
days you will walk into an airport lounge
and into my arms. I've waited like the
herons wait for the fish to appear in the
shallows near their feet, but unlike the
herons, I have doubts. What will I do?
My heart tells me my mind will tell me
everything. Part of me is as confident
as the heron. You will be nervous, too.
It is beyond my powers now, as much
as a poem is, but like writing a poem, I
know how to prepare for love. What else
do all his hidden messages mean but that:
prepare yourself? Not only the making
of beds and schedules; prepare words you
wish to tell him in Russian. It is your
life, your love, your heart whole you give.

Judy Hogan

Let the rest recede. Let your spirit be clear
and undivided, as still in its constancy as
the rock washed by cold, restless river water.
This wouldn't be happening to you if you
couldn't do it. You have worked through
your doubts. Let them go. Let the river
carry them like fragile leaf boats to the sea.
Time returns him into your arms. You
deserve this. Call it Life's gift, Life's
biggest prize awarded to the long-distance
runner who accepts the labor and the trouble;
who flies past the doubts until only the
essential things are in view. If the holy is
to arrive, you must let your heart be purified,
rinsed, and dried of its tears. This is the
best that waits: the very best there is.

This River

Twenty Five

I am here, and you are there, more than
before, since you did not walk off the plane
and into my arms, though I looked and looked
every time the one way door was opened
with a secret key by some airport official.
It helped to write you a letter yesterday,
though I hope to see you long before it
reaches there. Here by my river the hearts-
a-busting bush clings still to its orange seeds.
The maples are splashed with orange, red,
yellow. The other shore glows with the colors
I wrote you about last year. You are there,
and I can't read what is in your heart.
I study old poems for signs. I cut the
ivy on the path behind my house and pick
my way slowly over trees that have
fallen since I went that way last. The
morning glories are a glorious blue in
the garden that settles itself for winter.
A dog I don't know followed me here.
Our old dog died, took herself to the woods
and never returned. This dog is young
and chases around me, barking and leaping,

Judy Hogan

splashing into the cold river for a drink.
He lies quietly in the leaves, his eyes on me.
Another creature who reads me, as the geese
do, the herons, and even the fish; as you do.
Can you hear me whispering, "I love you,"
as I lean my cheek to the oaks, river birches,
and maples?
                        There's silver light in the
nearly black water on every ripple, every
edge. The sun is breaking above us. Whatever
despair we feel is silvered with hope. You
are coming. I believe that. You said so.
Now there is emptiness where my belief
was so strong when I went to meet the plane
which did not have you on the passenger list.
I'm more ready now. I've won my heart's
battle. I can love without fear, shame, or guilt.
There are two realities–inside and outside of
time. What we have is beyond time, but I want
to see you come through the door that opens
for you when you're on the other side. I
want to run to you, smiling, hear you say,
"Da, da, da. I'm here."

This River

Twenty Six

All the leaves of my life have fallen into
this river, most of them upside down, and
are floating slowly upstream. When
the rains do come, as the rains will, they'll
be rushed downstream. Then it will be my
turn to swim in earnest against the current.
I'm not afraid any more. It's all right now
for all my leaves to fall. I will put their
clear yellow into poems; how they change
the quality of the light all around them,
holding it like an aura, without any grasping
or imprisoning motion. As I walked here
to my favorite rock, the red leaves reached
out of me: "Take me, tell my story, let me
be memorized on the inner retina of your
eye." I took one and then another. I couldn't
take them all, but they all wanted to come
with me. Even the heron acts different.
He has settled in a pine about thirty feet
from me. He hides among the needles
but pokes his long beaked face out to have
a look. He makes his throaty sound, as if
crooning to himself or to me. He must

Judy Hogan

have used it to quiet his young ones; it's
such a comforting sound for one whose
main cry is a great sharp, raucous squawk,
as if you'd "done it" now by entering his world.
It has taken him five years to deign to sit
on this side of the river when I'm over here.
He learned to recognize me and didn't bother
to squawk; he sailed quietly away, to be
on the safe side. Then he let me see him
fishing. These past months I've watched
him and his family wading the shallows.
Now he flies so near that I see just how
thin, gaunt, and ill-proportioned he is.
He knows I love him. He has read
my heart, but it took him five years to
believe what he read. He's sleeping in
his den of pine brushes. He has crooned
himself to sleep. He trusts me that much,
just as you did, as these leaves do, letting
the lightest of breezes take them, tumbling
and turning, to the ground, or to float,
however they land, on the dark green
surface of the water. The water is jubilant.
It likes all these soft flat shapes, their
browns, yellows, and greens, the white
undersides, too, with an occasional splash

This River

of red. "We're on our way, then," it croons
to them, as a Skipper to a whole fleet of
ships. "The wind is insistent. Today
we're going upstream."

I, too, choose up.
The current I must make myself to move
against the larger stream where I live.
These newly fallen leaves are my
companions. They are not sorry any more
than I. We have all heard and believed
the crooning heron, who sees farther than
we do and crosses our slow passage on
strong wings every day of his life. He's
so sure of our reaching our destination–
the only one we wanted–that he sleeps,
and the wind that blows up quickly,
confidently over the water on this day
when we finally found the courage to cast
off, is the gentlest and wisest of guides.
Only the white clouds still share their
sky image with the water, rippled now to
look like watered silk. Behind me
the sun glints its reminder, that I am
only human; that's why it took me so long
to believe your words and my own heart,
the full meaning my life was able to be.

Judy Hogan

My dreams are charged in a new way.
Instead of moving toward them, I move
out from them. They are within. They
are me. Paradox is only part of what it is.
The part that matters is as eternal as sun
glinting on the slight surface the water is
able to raise above the level of all the
other water because of a little wind. When
everything in you has made itself ready and
your leaves hang golden and willing, even
eager, to fall at a touch, then all it takes
is a breath. The breath is given. Most
of the water being pushed faster now is
brown, but I see the clouds still, their clarity,
their white, and the blue depths between.

This River

Twenty Seven

You would have been sitting here, seeing
the last red glow of the maples, a few oranges
and yellows. Almost everything is brown
now, though the grass is green, and the
honeysuckle vines. In the woods, layered
with brown leaves, wet and shiny after days
of cold rain, there are green ferns, self-heal,
and wild ginger. I brought in flowers before
the frost came, and unripe tomatoes, which
turn red in the dark. The black-eyed susans
let go their unruly medusa mops of green
twisted petals, relax, and open, one by one.
Each petal was folded in three–the
undersides are green, the flower is yellow.
The green center turns brown. This takes
weeks. I celebrate each new uncovering
of silken gold, each further flush of bristling
brown in the bald green center where seeds
form.
       I move closer to believing you'll come.
I get a message: you plan to come in ten days.
But your plan requires many pieces to work
for you. The first main piece has failed. If
you arrive, it will be a miracle, but I believe
in miracles where you and I are concerned.

Judy Hogan

I can see the river from this desk I fixed for you.
It runs brown and fast today. All weekend
we've had cold rain. I've kept warm with
last year's logs and the piece of dead branch
they finally took down in honor of your
coming. I've soothed myself with these
petals opening. There is almost a full
sun now to shine inside when the winter
sun hides himself with blank grey skies,
and you are held there by difficulties I
can not imagine, though I feel your ingenuity
at work. I count the open petals and the
closed green ones. The yellow ones are
winning. Your plan is bold. Only I am up
to you. The others are frightened. They
tell me all the reasons I should be afraid, too,
but they don't have this spun gold between,
which you and I have. It reaches easily
over the ocean, floating upriver even on
a dark, grey day, when the rains have
swollen the current, turned it brown, and
it rushes seaward in an agony of destination-
consciousness. But you send gold.

This River

I receive the message: the yellow narcissus
of March resurrect themselves in November,
one gold petal at a time. I am ready for you,
whether we lie together in love or not, marry
or not, and then my mind sends me my own
nightmare of debate. I know all my
disbeliefs by heart and all the answers as
well. The answer of answers is the hardest
to hear: you love me. You speak any way
you can, through gold opening itself, one
fold at a time, through the envelope with
its single rose, through the messages
conveyed by two or more people. The child
in me, the lonely woman, and the writer–
they all want this love you give me,
persistently, boldly, tenderly.
Consummation is delayed. But without
doubt there is love. It's why I have been
faithful*, and my *calm* has stayed inside me.
I have let myself stay *beautiful*. You
convinced me I was *kind*. You saw it like
a yellow light around me. I rise to the
occasion. Even your absence gives me
new visions, of how our love twines itself
like gold in illuminated manuscripts
through the pages I write and will write.

Judy Hogan

The future's huge dark spaces lies ahead
of us, starless above us. My mind woke
me at two a.m. to tell me: "Fill the space
with what you want. It's up to you."
I choose everything again: this house,
its hill, my garden, this village, this river,
my work, my children and friends, and
my hope to live with you one day, to
speak your language well. I choose all
my conflicts, all my responsibilities,
gladly. We will fill this huge space
that opens. This is the *truth*. I will end
by being *wise* and knowing how to *love*.

* *all words in italics* attributed to Penelope, wife of Odysseus. In ancient Greek legends, she was ever faithful to her husband.

This River

Twenty Eight

I keep expecting brown, all brown, but the woods
give me gold and red. Even in the black water
gold beech leaves, red dogwood, as if these leaves
held onto their colors to welcome you, wanted
you to see them hanging low and red at the edge,
blurred by the ripples the wind sends, yet they
glow there. Farther out the river holds the dark
blue of the sky. We have sun in November and
the russet colors of oak, the yellow light in the
sycamores, their leaves lacy with the holes some
insect has made. All these leaves are waiting
for you. The wind hasn't loosened their hold.
As long as they can, they'll stay gold and red.
I have more to give you since I made my peace
with the writing I must do for life. It's outrageous
to love you, but that's how I am. Your letting
me know your love in all the hundred subtle
ways you invent to do that has finally quieted
me. I can be serene, as Dante was when he
contemplated his Beatrice. I may be the first
woman to be so bold as to proclaim that
my love is good and holy. Time will tell
what I will suffer, but I'm ready for that, too.

Judy Hogan

None of the others I've loved has wanted
me to know he loved me back. You keep
risking yourself to give me that knowledge.
You loved me first. You were bold when
I was afraid. You insisted I suffer, too.
I gave you that, and I will again. You have
me for life. Plain words, sealed with heart's
truth. Its colors are red and gold. Red
for our blood; gold for the threads our souls
spin, no matter how far they must reach,
like those spiders that send a strand fifteen
feet across a clearing. How do they find
the courage? Why do they even try?
They do it for love. For you I would walk
right into death. But I don't think we'll
die just yet. Living the difficulties as
you do now, trying to get here, as we will,
too, when you're here and we see things
differently–that's where the real courage starts.
I will summon red leaves then and remember
the day I anticipated brown, and the river
kept giving me red in the shallows, and across,
on the other side, gold, when the wind died,

This River

and more gold. The sun is no less emphatic,
making even the black water dance with gold
light, singing a Russian tune, spinning and
turning, dizzy with gold.

Judy Hogan

Twenty Nine

The red and gold are gone, lodged in memory,
but the water has deepened its blue, the tree
limbs are whiter; the river laps eagerly,
lovingly, tenderly at the rocks that define
its banks. One rock higher, I feel such urgent
desire it's as if you spoke to me out of old
letters, out of my poems. I've given you
voice there, put words I could hear into
your mouth. Sometimes it was the heron
or the river itself that reminded me what
I do know, have known, that goes back to
five days spent in your presence, when we
made our vows silently. You spoke your
feelings aloud once when we were alone,
but I couldn't translate. My heart did its
own translation, whatever the words you
said. Those few, simple ones, said with
a broken, emphatic sound, torn by their roots
out of your soul--my soul knew right away
what you meant. We've been planning
our future ever since. It's a long way off,
but you will walk into my arms–beloved!

This River

The water in the shallows is so dark
that it often deceives us. It's the look
upriver we must practice, especially
on a clear winter day like today when
the winter solstice is days away, and
the undaunted sun illumines the black
water behind us. Faith in our good
fortune must keep hope alive, no matter
how circumstances turn to trap us. We
have the only thing needful to outwit
the gods and make them our servants:
that deep look into each other's eyes,
which takes us straight into the Universe's
heart and releases every kind of bondage.
Against the link we've forged, no chains
will prevail, no sorrow kill us with its
grey ash, its bitter tears. Joy grows,
persistent, out of the soil we stand on.
This field in winter looks barren. Here,
it's brown. The leaves have let their
color go. Brown finally claimed them.
There, snow layers the field where we
found a purple flower to celebrate our
meeting–one little knapweed bloom was
all you needed to make you stretch
your arms wide and give me your soul.

Judy Hogan

Don't be surprised if you find a purple
flower blooming in the snow. Here,
where brown claims all, there is still
gold dancing toward me from downstream,
giving me the music of your voice,
your laughter, and in the woods are
red berries on the holly. Honeysuckle
twines its green way up tree trunks,
hanging dark blue berries out to shine
in winter light; the cedar's fronds
are festive, too, with dots of bright blue.
What grows out of our souls' soil is safe.
We will tuck what we have into the wall
of the centuries, filling the cracks with
our words full of wisdom and hope.
It's love our planet's people must learn.
It often begins in hate. Whomever we
thought we hated we can learn to love.
We can learn to take the anger we feel
for the other and claim it as our own.
We hate that the other isn't perfect,
fails to know what we feel, scares us
with threats. Even the terrorist is trying
to do what is right. Anger is desire
gone bad like sour milk. This we can

This River

bake into bread, make into cakes. If
we are busy feeding each other, we
won't have time to hate.
                      I don't feel
"good enough" for the love you bear
me. But I know I'm as good as people
get. Right now I'm as naked to your
seeing as these winter boughs. I have
no disguises for you, from you. You'll
see straight in. It's how I see you, too.
The shallows will give us trouble,
and the rocks along the bank, but not
the blue depths smiling back at me
today from upriver. We journey there
easily enough–in time and out of time,
loving our fate into existence as best
we can, living out one human cycle,
two lifetimes, completely.

Judy Hogan

Thirty

Three solstices since I saw you; we move
toward summer. The trees whir with
migrating birds dining on last year's seeds.
The shadow trees, their beaver-gnawed limbs,
their sweetgum balls, are rippled, then calm.
The image imprints itself faster than the wind
blurs the outline. Water moves, the earth
moves, I move, our love moves. Nothing
stays still. The beavers are half-way through
another tree. The river erases its tree
shadows and bears its blue tide toward me.
It holds only sky now and whatever the sky
holds. It flashes its watery light along the
rock; the naked limbs in the beaver cove
dance. The trees separate from the water.
A wind is all it takes.
                         River water
foretold your coming. To the river I've
returned week after week to learn of the
love that lives and runs in my soul. I've
read all the messages of the dancing light,
the leaves falling and floating; I've studied
the labors of the beaver. I've never seen her,
only the felled trees, the stripped bark,
the sapling limbs piled up in the shallows.

This River

The river still waits for us, as it waits for
the beaver. But the labor to live by its side,
in its ken, is immense. It will take all
our wits, all our truthfulness, all our
patience from now till the end of our lives.
For the living the green light in the blood,
the sun's dazzle on the water, comes and
goes; is faint and then clear. The clear
days are easy. I hold them within me
stored like sun under ice. It's the deep
black water that separates us, soul from
soul. Seeing light gleam there is an
act of the laborer within the soul; its
beaver spirit, which wakes in the
dead of night and returns to gnaw
at the still unfelled tree. Each tree
that falls may fall wrong; may get hung
in other branches; may never touch
the cove which was what the beaver
planned for. But gnaw enough trees
enough times, and some will land where
you want them to and sustain your body
and soul for days. It's hard to remember.

Judy Hogan

It hurts to miss you. Belief is numbed
by delay. But memory lifts up your
promises. My knowledge of your love
swims back into view. It's far over
there on the other side of the island,
with a whole winter river, pale and
then dark with the other shore's shadow
between. It's only a line of light–
a slender dazzling cord of silver.
It doesn't feed me or touch me, smile
or speak. It has no arms, no laughter.
No tears. It doesn't suffer as far as I
know. But it returns. It helps me wait.
It turns my mind back to minutes which
passed by the side of another river
more than three solstices ago. Your
words poured into me straight, and I
couldn't ward them off. You were
already grieving at losing me, and I'd
just arrived. Your words loved me
until I surrendered. The pulse in
my blood began to move, and I knew
then my fate. We left time then.
That's what the light can do when
it silvers the radiant water–no matter
how far away. It can lift our souls

This River

free of time. But only if we take
lessons from the beaver and continue
our nocturnal labors. The wind
that brings the light over there takes
away the tree shadows in the cove;
the intricate patterns even of awkward
and broken trees. Our souls see the
beauty when the light returns because
we foreknew it in the black depths
of the night. Better to aim one's
life toward a radiant horizon, a sky
made red by sun, than let oblivion
declare black the sole reality, or, grey,
our fated life. The river keeps brimming
with gold. My eyes keep seeing the
glowing embers of a sky in winter
before the dark curtain falls.

Judy Hogan

"Heart L eaves"

drawing by
Mikhail Bazankov

(Михаил Фёдорович Базанков)

This River

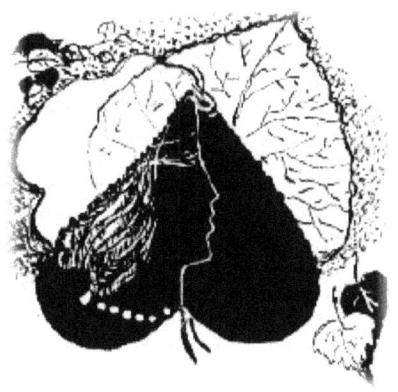

Judy Hogan

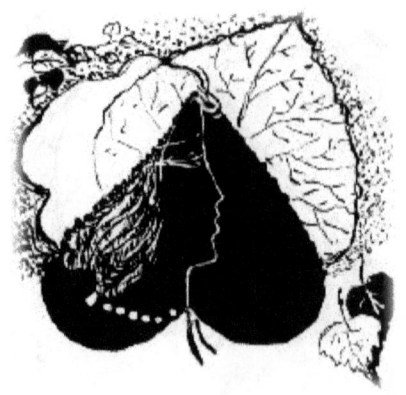

This River

Gratitude

I would like to thank my editor/publisher antoinette nora claypoole of *Wild Embers Press* and their *Watersongs* imprint for her belief in this book. Also thanks to Doug Williams for assistance with photo of book cover art, Natalya Ilyina and Yevstolia Rumyantsev for details of Sergei Rumyantsev biography and Russian name linguistics, and the Rumyantsev family for their generous permission to use his artwork for the book cover.

Others have also gathered around to support its coming into print: poet Sharon and her husband John Ewing, who hosted visiting Russian writers and a painter from Kostroma many times and visited Kostroma with me in 1995; poet Foster Robertson Foreman, once a co-publisher of *Hyperion Poetry Journal* with me and her husband Paul; poet Joanie McLean, poet and journalist Susan Broili, who traveled to Kostroma with me in 1992, and poet Jaki Shelton Green, who helped us with *Earth and Soul: An Anthology of North Carolina Poetry*, in a dual language edition.

This River, Six in was originally published in *Beaver Soul* by *Finishing Line Press* of Kentucky *(2013) and* in Russian by The Kostroma Writers Organization (1997). *Six* was translated into Russian by Galina Gamper of St. Petersburg.

I especially thank Mikhail Bazankov and all my other good Russian friends who made my time in Russia so enjoyable and rewarding and who liked my poems and took my role of poet so seriously that they often stopped what they were doing to read my poems on the spot. A special thanks to Mikhail's family, who took me into their home, shared their village life with me, and helped me understand Russian cultural ways.

Permissions

"Heart Leaves" artwork, Mikhail Bazankov.
Cover Art (study of Volga River) by Sergei Rumyantsev. family of Sergei Rumyantsev.
"Grow in Spirit", Edmund Keeley translation of Cavafy, Edmund Keeley

Judy Hogan

About the Artists

photo credit: Art-Katalog.com

Sergei Rumyantsev
Сергей Румянцев

Sergei Sergeevich Rumyantsev (1928-2013) painter, was born in the former Soviet Union, in the village of Zavrazhye, Parfenevskogo district, Kostroma region.

Judy Hogan

In 1953 he graduated from a military school in Baku, Azerbaijan, worked in the militia, then "in the sphere of culture in a small city of the Kostroma region". Yevstolia Rumyantsev, Sergei's w i f e explains: "All this time he drew, painted and was an active and successful participant of amateur art exhibitions. Soon he understood that art was his true inclination and turned to painting. He was a self-taught painter and also played the guitar." Rumyantsev graduated in 1959 from an art correspondence course of University of Arts, the Moscow institute named after Nadezhda "Nadya" Konstantinovna Krupskaya Наде́жда Константи́новна Кру́пская. *(translated/written by Natalya Ilyina-- Kostroma, Russia-- from notes to author/editor, Oct. 2014).*

Becoming a member of the (Soviet) Union of Artists in 1968, Rumyantsev served as a committee member jurying art exhibitions in fifteen regions of Russia. In 2008 he received a silver medal from the Russian Academy of Fine Arts and in that same year a book of his rememberings and stories coupled with a disc of Russian folk songs in which he performed was released: *It's Me, People.* According to Yevstolia, "a new book (2014) of his paintings is ready but has not yet been published."

Rumyantsev's Russian museum collections include, Kaliningrad State Art Gallery, Kostroma State Art Museum; Yaroslavl Art Museum and his work can be viewed and found for sale on the web (2014) at http://www.art-katalog.com/english/painter/667.

This River

Mikhail Fedorovich Bazankov

Михаил Фёдорович Базанков*

"Mikhail Bazankov was born in October 1937 in a small village in the Mezha district of the Kostroma Region in Russia. He married his wife Katya when they were both young, and they have two grown sons and several grandchildren.

Judy Hogan

Mikhail was trained as a painter, but his novel *Memory Has Rights, Too* achieved national publication in 1986, and he joined the Soviet Union of Writers. His novels and children's books have been widely read. By 1990 he was President of the Kostroma Writers Organization in Kostroma, the region's capital. He then edited and published many Kostroma writers in single books and in anthologies. He traveled the region, working with writers in remote areas. Between 1990 and 1995 he worked with Judy Hogan on five exchange visits of writers between Durham *[North Carolina]* and Kostroma through the Sister Cities of Durham organization and also helped in 1998 with the painter Nikolai Smirnov's visit to Durham and his art exhibit there. "

~*~ Bio written by Judy Hogan ~*~

* "Also spelled Михаил Фёдорович Базанков. When Russians pronounce the first two letters in the patronymic 'Фёдорович' they sound as in the word 'fur' or 'fir' in English, but in writing the letter ' ё ' loses the upper ' ¨ ' and turns into 'e'. That's why sometimes you see 'Федорович' and sometimes 'Фёдорович'. Both are right." ~~Note from Natalya Ilyina *(to editor, Oct.*

This River

About the Poet

photo by Mark Schmerling.

Judy Hogan

In the mid-late 1960's Judy Hogan was studying the Classics as a graduate student at University of California, Berkeley. Following those studies, she moved back East and has lived in the Triangle area of North Carolina, bringing to the state a new poetry journal (*Hyperion*, 1970-81) and in 1976 founding *Carolina Wren Press*.

Judy Hogan

Judy has written six books of poetry including a chapbook, *Beaver Soul*, published by *Finishing Line Press* in 2013. It was originally published in Russian by the Kostroma Writers' Organization in 1997. Mystery novels in her *Penny Weaver* series include *Farm Fresh and Fatal* (2013) and *Killer Frost* (2012), both published by *Mainly Murder Press*.

Chair of COSMEP (*Committee of Small Magazine Editors and Publishers*) from 1975-78, in 1984 she helped found and was the first President of the North Carolina Writers' Network, serving until 1987. She has been active in environmental issues in her region since the early 1970's, serving the community as a reviewer, book distributor, publisher, teacher, writing consultant, organizer of readings, book signing events, and conferences.

Between 1990 and 2007 Judy visited Kostroma, Russia, five times, teaching American literature at Kostroma University in 1995 and presenting a paper on *Spirituality in the Work of Anna Akhmatova* to a Kostroma University Literature Conference in March 2007. Between 1990 and 2001, she worked on five Sister Cities exchange visits, cooperatively published North Carolina and Kostroma writers, and assisted exchanges with Kostroma visual artists. She has taught all forms of creative writing for forty years, does free lance editing for creative writers and offers workshops. Literary and personal papers, correspondence, and twenty-five years of Judy Hogan's extensive diaries can be found in the Sallie Bingham Collection of Women's History and Culture, Perkins Library, Duke University, Durham, North Carolina.

Judy lives and farms in Moncure, N.C., near the Haw River and Jordan Lake.

This River

www.ingramcontent.com/pod-product-compliance
Lightning Source LLC
Chambersburg PA
CBHW061448040426
42450CB00007B/1274